best
easy
day hikes
Orange County

Randy Vogel

D1053776

FALCONGUIDES ®

GUILFORD, CONNECTICUT
HELENA, MONTANA

AN IMPRINT OF THE GLOBE PEQUOT PRESS

FALCONGUIDES®

Copyright © 1999 Morris Book Publishing, LLC
Previously published by Falcon Publishing Inc.

FalconGuides is an imprint of The Globe Pequot Press.
Falcon and FalconGuides are registered trademarks of Morris Book
Publishing, LLC.

Library of Congress Cataloging-in-Publication Data
Vogel, Randy.
    Best easy day hikes, Orange County / Randy Vogel.
        p.   cm. — (A Falcon guide)
    ISBN 978-1-56044-865-5
    1. Hiking—California—Orange County Guidebooks 2. Orange County
(Calif.) Guidebooks.   I. Title.   II. Series.
GV199.42.C220738   1999
917.94'960453—dc21   99-34382
                                                                CIP

Printed in Canada
First Edition/Fifth Printing

Contents

Acknowledgments

I would like to thank my wife Sarah for her assistance in gathering information for this guide and accompanying me while conducting field research. I also would like to acknowledge the help of my daughter Claire, who endured (and enjoyed) many of these hikes, often in less than ideal weather conditions. Lastly, I wish to thank Orange County Harbors, Beaches, and Parks employees Jeff Dickman and Tim Miller, who have previously provided me with considerable assistance regarding Orange County wilderness and regional park trails.

Map Legend

Interstate	(00)	Campground	▲
US Highway	(00)	Picnic Area	🪑
State or Other Principal Road	(00) (000)	Cabins/Buildings	■
Forest Road	416	Peak	9,782 ft.
Interstate Highway or Other Freeway	⟹	Elevation	9,782 ft. ✕
Paved Road	⟹	River/Creek/ Waterfall	
Gravel Road	⟹	Marsh	↯
Unimproved Road	====⟹	Gate	•—
Trailhead	◯	Bridge/Dam	)(
Parking Area	Ⓟ	Mine Site	✗
Main Trail/Route	•••—•—	Overlook/Point of Interest	◧
Main Trail/Route on Dirt Road	⟋⟋⟋	National Forest/Park Boundary	⌐ ¬
Alternate/Secondary Trail/Route	-•-•-•-	County Boundary	
Alternate/Secondary Trail/Route on Dirt Road	⟋⟋⟋	Map Orientation	N ◆
Direction of Travel	⇄	Scale	0 0.5 1 Miles
City	◯		

Overview Map of Orange County

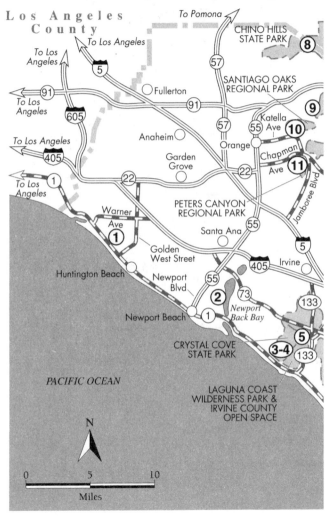

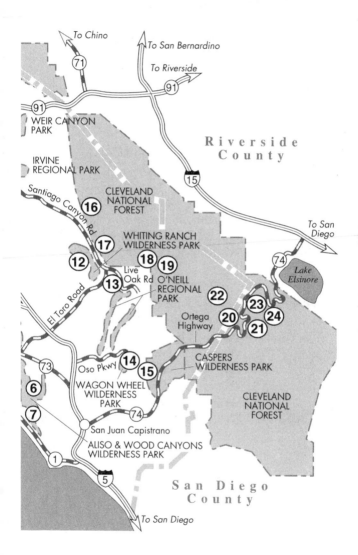

Ranking the Hikes

The following list ranks the hikes in each section of this book from easiest to hardest.

The Coast

Easiest

1. Bolsa Chica Slough Trail
2. Upper Newport Bay Trail
7. Valido Trail
5. Laurel Canyon–Bommer Ridge Loop
3. No Name Ridge–Moro Canyon Loop
4. East Cut-Across to Moro Ridge Loop

Hardest 6. West Ridge, Lynx, and Cholla Trails

The Foothills

Easiest

10. Santiago Creek Trail Loop
11. Peters Canyon Lake Loop
14. Wagon Wheel Park Loop
15. West Ridge and Oak Trail Loop
13. Live Oak Trail
8. Telegraph Canyon via Rimcrest Entrance
9. Weir Canyon Trail Loop

Hardest 12. Borrego Canyon to Red Rock Canyon

The Mountains

Introduction

Orange County is fortunate to have a large amount of open space and hiking opportunities. However, many of our open spaces remain threatened by development and toll road construction. Our county parks, state parks, and national forests are threatened by declining budgets and skyrocketing visitation.

In addition to following the Leave No Trace guidelines found in this guide, consider supporting groups and organizations that help preserve and maintain parks and trails. I urge you to join Trails4All, a nonprofit organization dedicated to preserving Orange County parks and maintaining its trails. You may contact them by writing to 300 North Flower Street, P.O. Box 4048, Santa Ana, CA 92702, or at www.trails4all.org.

A note on timing: To approximate how long it will take you to complete a given trail described in this guide, use the standard of two miles per hour, adding time if you are not a strong hiker or are traveling with small children, and subtracting time if you are in good shape. Add time for picnics, rest stops, or other activities you plan for your outing.

I've listed the pertinent U.S. Geological Survey 7.5-minute topographical maps with each hike for your reference. Other maps of the areas described herein can be found through the USDA Forest Service; the Orange County Harbors, Beaches, and Parks Department; and at respective state parks.

— *Randy Vogel*

Zero Impact

The trails that weave through Orange County parks and the Cleveland National Forest are heavily used, and sometimes take a real beating. Because of their proximity to pollution and dense population we, as trail users and advocates, must be especially vigilant to make sure our passing leaves no lasting mark. If we all leave our mark on the landscape, the parks and wildlands eventually will be despoiled.

These trails can accommodate plenty of human travel if everybody treats them with respect. Just a few thoughtless, badly mannered, or uninformed visitors can ruin them for everyone who follows.

The Zero-Impact Principles

- *Leave with everything you brought with you.*
- *Leave no sign of your visit.*
- *Leave the landscape as you found it.*

Litter is the scourge of all trails. It is unsightly, polluting, and potentially dangerous to wildlife. Pack out all your own trash, including biodegradable items like orange peels, which might be sought out by area critters. You should also pack out garbage left trailside by less considerate hikers. Store a plastic bag in your pack to use for trash removal.

Don't approach or feed any wild creatures—the ground squirrel eyeing your snack food is best able to survive if it remains self-reliant, because it is not likely to find cookies along the trail when winter comes.

Never pick flowers, or gather plants or insects. So many people visit these trails that the cumulative effect of even small impacts can be great.

Stay on established trails. Shortcutting and cutting switchbacks promotes erosion. Select durable surfaces, like rocks, logs, or sandy areas, for resting spots.

Most of the trails described in this guide are also used by horseback riders and mountain bikers. Acquaint yourself with proper trail etiquette and be courteous. When possible, hikers should step to the side of the trail to allow horses and bicyclists to pass. Learn to share the trail with other users. Be courteous by not making loud noises while hiking. Consider volunteering time to trail maintenance projects, giving something back to the parks and trails you enjoy.

If possible, use outhouses at trailheads or along the trail. If not, pack in a lightweight trowel and a plastic bag so that you can bury your waste 6 to 8 inches deep. Pack out used toilet paper in a plastic bag. Make sure you relieve yourself at least 300 feet away from any surface water or boggy spot, and off any established trail.

Remember to abide by the golden rule of backcountry travel: If you pack it in, pack it out! Keep your impact to a minimum; taking only pictures and leaving only footprints.

Put your ear to the ground and listen carefully. Thousands of people coming behind you are thankful for your courtesy and good sense.

Play It Safe

Generally, hiking in Orange County is a safe and fun way to explore the outdoors. Though there are no guarantees, there is much you can do to help ensure each outing is a safe and enjoyable one. Below, you'll find an abbreviated list of hiking do's and don'ts, but by no means should this list be considered comprehensive. You are strongly encouraged to verse yourself in the art of backcountry travel. You should also consider learning more about the flora, fauna, and geology of Southern California, which will greatly enhance your enjoyment and appreciation of these hikes. A good outdoor specialty store is a great place to begin.

Know the basics of first aid, including how to treat bleeding, bites and stings, and fractures, strains, or sprains. Few of the hikes are so remote that help can't be reached within a short time, but you would be wise to carry and know how to use simple supplies, such as over-the-counter pain relievers, bandages, and ointments. Pack a first-aid kit on each excursion.

Familiarize yourself with the symptoms of both cold and heat-related conditions, including hypothermia and particularly heat stroke. The best way to avoid these afflictions is to wear clothing appropriate to the weather conditions, drink plenty of fluids, eat enough, and keep a pace that is within your physical limits.

Protect yourself from excessive exposure to sun by wearing a hat and using sunscreen. During the summer, avoid hiking during the middle of the day when temperatures can reach more than 100 degrees F. Early mornings are cooler and birds and other wildlife are more active and more readily observed.

The hills and mountains are home to a variety of wildlife, from squirrels to mountain lions. Squirrels can be host to disease and mountain lions may attack if prompted by hunger. Rattlesnakes may be found on any of the hikes described, particularly from early spring to mid-fall. Watch where you put your hands and feet. If given a chance, most rattlesnakes will try to avoid a confrontation.

Poison oak is common throughout Orange County's hills, valleys, and mountains. Know how to identify this distinctive three-leaved plant and avoid all contact. Even the bare branches should be avoided.

Ticks are another pest to be avoided. They hang in the brush waiting to drop on warm-blooded animals (people included). Check for ticks and remove any before they have a chance to bite.

Most free-flowing water should be considered unsafe to drink if untreated. Bring all the water you need with you.

Whether short and easy or long and strenuous, you'll enjoy each of these hikes much more if you wear good socks and appropriate footwear. Carry a comfortable day pack containing ample water, snacks and/or lunch, and extra clothing. Maps are not necessary, but they are fun to have along. Bring other items to increase your enjoyment of the hike, such as a camera, a manual to help identify plants and wildflowers, and binoculars.

The Coast

The coastal areas of Orange County range from sandy beaches and tidal estuaries in the north to rocky shorelines and rugged coastal hills to the south. Accordingly, the hiking experiences along Orange County's coast vary considerably. Bolsa Chica and Newport Bay feature easy walks with ample wildlife viewing, perfect for a short family outing. Crystal Cove State Park, Laguna Coast Wilderness Park, and Aliso & Wood Canyons Wilderness Park offer longer and more challenging hikes into the coastal hills and canyons.

The coastal areas of Orange County are also some of the most threatened and biologically important in California. Estuaries and wetlands are probably the most ecologically diverse and fertile areas on the planet, but are disappearing at an alarming rate. Most of these areas have fallen victim to housing developments or have been dredged to create marinas. Coastal hills, once covered in native coastal sage and other unique plant communities, are being graded to make way for toll roads and housing subdivisions, which are ubiquitous in southern Orange County. Still, Orange County has saved small remnants of this landscape, and this guide will direct you to some of the most accessible and spectacular scenery remaining.

Bolsa Chica Slough Trail

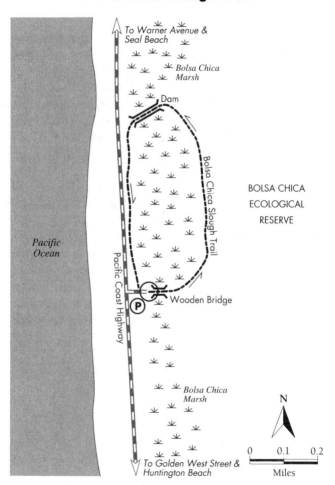

To Warner Avenue & Seal Beach

Bolsa Chica Marsh

Dam

Pacific Ocean

Pacific Coast Highway

Bolsa Chica Slough Trail

BOLSA CHICA ECOLOGICAL RESERVE

P

Wooden Bridge

Bolsa Chica Marsh

To Golden West Street & Huntington Beach

N

0   0.1   0.2
Miles

8

1
BOLSA CHICA SLOUGH TRAIL

Type of hike: Loop.
Total distance: 1.5 miles.
Elevation gain: 15 feet.
Jurisdiction: Bolsa Chica Ecological Reserve.
Finding the trailhead: Take either Warner Avenue or Golden West Street west from Interstate 405 (the San Diego Freeway) to the Pacific Coast Highway (PCH/California 1). From Warner Avenue, head about 1.5 miles south on the PCH. From Golden West Street, drive north on the PCH for approximately 2.5 miles. Park in the small parking lot on the inland (east) side of the PCH. The lot is nearly opposite the entrance to Bolsa Chica State Beach.

Key points:
0.1 Dirt trail begins on far side of bridge.
0.8 Reach the northern apex of the trail at the seawater inlet.
1.5 Return to the starting point at the parking lot.

The hike: For many years the Bolsa Chica Ecological Reserve consisted of 530 acres of marsh and former marsh just inland from Pacific Coast Highway north of Huntington Beach. As this guide is being written, residents of Orange

County are celebrating the purchase of an additional 880 acres of wetlands that were once slated for dredging and construction of a marina. This reserve, and the wetlands farther north in the Seal Beach National Wildlife Refuge, are one of the last remaining and most important fresh-saltwater estuaries in Southern California. Binoculars are a must, as you will have the opportunity to see a wide variety of birds. Terns, plovers, avocets, herons, egrets, various migratory sparrows, marsh hawks, and cormorants are only a few of the variety of avian life to be seen. In the future, surrounding wetlands will be restored, oil drilling equipment removed, and hiking and wildlife viewing opportunities dramatically increased.

Begin the hike by taking the long wooden bridge over the shallow marshlands. On the opposite side of the bridge at 0.1 mile, follow the dirt trail as it works its way to the left (north), then atop an old levee. Interpretive signs will help you identify wildlife.

The trail continues northward along levees on the inland side of the main, restored tidal marshlands. Note how different species of birds seek different types of food or use differing search strategies. Beak size and shape play a role in their hunting techniques.

At 0.8 mile, you will reach the northern apex of the trail, and will pass over an inlet for seawater into the marsh. Now you are heading south, the marsh on your left and the coastal highway and Pacific Ocean beyond to your right. Depending on the time of year and time of day, the species and activity of the bird life will vary. Continue south along the marsh's edge until you return to the parking lot at 1.5 miles.

2
UPPER NEWPORT BAY TRAIL

Type of hike: Loop.
Total distance: 1.7 miles.
Elevation gain: 50 feet.
Topo map: USGS Newport Beach.
Jurisdiction: Upper Newport Bay Ecological Reserve.
Finding the trailhead: From California 55 (the Newport Freeway), take Bristol Boulevard south to Irvine/Campus (the street changes its name). From Interstate 405 (the San Diego Freeway), take MacArthur Boulevard south to Irvine/Campus. Head west on Irvine/Campus for about 2 miles to Santiago Drive. Turn left (southwest) onto Santiago, proceed one block south to Constellation Avenue, and turn left (west). Constellation Avenue is a small dead-end street; park here. The trail begins at the end of the street.

Key points:
0.2 Cross the first bridge.
0.3 Cross the second bridge.
0.7 Head up the gully to the bluff top.
1.3 Descend from the bluff to the second bridge.

The hike: Upper Newport Bay is one of the most valuable saltwater marshes in Southern California, and is home to hundreds of species of fish, birds, and native plants. Though often viewed by some as "wastelands," fresh and saltwater

11

Upper Newport Bay Trail

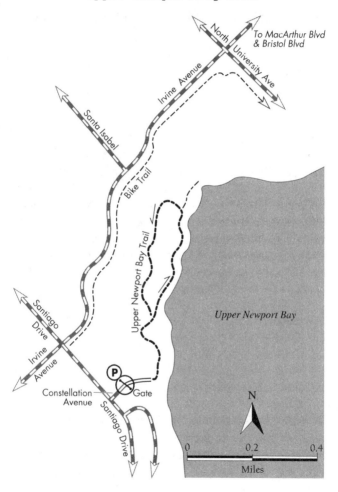

marshes, like those found in Upper Newport Bay, are some of the richest biological areas on the planet. The calm waters of the bay serve as breeding grounds for dozens of fish species, and migratory birds feed on the many types of fish, plants, and invertebrate animals. Public outcry and state funds helped preserve this resource, which was once slated for development into a marina and harbor community. Be sure to bring a good pair of binoculars, as dozens of rarely seen species of birds can be viewed from the trail. This loop hike follows dirt paths that first take you along the very edge of the marsh flats, then return atop the rim of the bluffs.

From the gate at the trailhead, proceed down a wide trail for about 100 yards, then make a left onto a footpath, following this path to the left above the bay's edge. As the trail curves left at 0.2 mile, you cross a small bridge near palm trees. A hundred yards further, take a right-hand fork, downhill. Cross another bridge at 0.3 mile to a three-way trail junction; stay right, and follow the footpath that proceeds along the very edge of the marsh. Stay right where a concrete drain is seen above and to the left.

You will continue along the marsh's rim until the trail again forks near a break in the bluffs. Proceed left behind bushes, then up the gully on an eroded path at 0.7 mile. Farther up the gully, head left, following a steep path to the top of the bluff. Turn left and proceed back south along the bluff's rim. By staying near the rim of the bluff, you have fine views of the bay and are following a well-traveled series of trails.

Eventually, the bluffs end and you drop down, joining your previous route near the second bridge crossing at 1.3 miles. Follow your route back to the parking area.

3
NO NAME RIDGE–MORO CANYON LOOP

Type of hike: Loop.
Total distance: 3.6 miles.
Elevation gain: 600 feet.
Topo map: USGS Laguna Ridge.
Jurisdiction: Crystal Cove State Park.
Finding the trailhead: To reach the No Name Ridge trailhead, take Laguna Canyon Road (California 133) south from either Interstate 5 (the Santa Ana Freeway) or Interstate 405 (the San Diego Freeway) to its terminus at the Pacific Coast Highway (PCH/California 1). Drive north on the PCH approximately 2.8 miles to El Moro Road, where you will find a traffic signal and an elementary school. Turn east (right), and drive up the road to the entrance booth (a right-hand turn). Either pay here or at the self-serve pay machine in the parking area a short distance ahead. The trailhead is at the east (far) end of the lot.

Key points:
0.9 Reach the summit of No Name Ridge.
1.5 Arrive at the West Cut-Across Trail junction.
2.3 Reach the floor of Moro Canyon.
3.6 The trail ends at the parking area.

No Name Ridge–Moro Canyon Loop

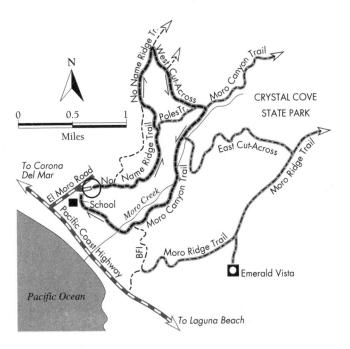

The hike: As you head up the No Name Ridge Trail on the northern side of Crystal Cove State Park, you will encounter views west to the ocean, north into Muddy Canyon and toward Los Trancos Canyon, east toward the ridge of the San Joaquin Hills, and south into Moro Canyon. Much—but alas, not all—of what the eye beholds is set to come into public ownership, preserving this habitat and open space for future generations. All the gradual uphills are rewarded with more than great views; from the apex of the hike, you descend directly into Moro Canyon, where winter and spring rains will have filled the creek and saturated the hillsides with many varieties of flowering plants.

Begin the hike by taking the No Name Ridge Trail as it heads east, uphill from the eastern end of the parking lot. The trail winds up the southern side of a large hillside, with views directly down into Moro Canyon and back toward the Pacific Ocean.

Stay left at the Poles Trail junction, continuing uphill until you reach the top of the hill at 0.9 mile. Here, you can manage fantastic views in all directions.

The trail makes two short descents and climbs before leveling out along the ridgeline. The well-marked junction with the West Cut-Across Trail is on your right (south) at 1.5 miles. Head right and downhill, following the West Cut-Across as it descends some 325 feet through open grasslands, eventually reaching the floor of Moro Canyon at 2.3 miles.

Head right (west) along the Moro Canyon Trail as it gently descends along the canyon bottom. Though well-traveled by foot, horse, and bicycle, you can well imagine being transported back 100 years or more. Wildflowers, birds, rabbits, and an occasional bobcat may be spied.

Eventually, the trail heads to the right (north) and uphill, back to the parking area and your starting point at 3.6 miles.

4
EAST CUT-ACROSS TO MORO RIDGE LOOP

Type of hike: Loop.
Total distance: 4.7 miles.
Elevation gain: 750 feet.
Topo map: USGS Laguna Beach.
Jurisdiction: Crystal Cove State Park.
Finding the trailhead: Take Laguna Canyon Road (California 133) south from Interstate 5 (the Santa Ana Freeway) or Interstate 405 (the San Diego Freeway) to its terminus at the Pacific Coast Highway (PCH/California 1). Drive north on the PCH for approximately 2.8 miles to El Moro Road, where you will find an elementary school and a traffic light. Turn right (east), and drive up the road to the entrance booth (a right-hand turn). Either pay here or at the self-serve pay machine in the parking area a short distance ahead. The trailhead is at the west end of the lot.

Key points:
0.4 The trail comes to the bottom of Moro Canyon.
1.5 Reach the East Cut-Across Trail junction.
2.5 The trail reaches the ridgetop and the Moro Ridge Trail.
3.2 Pass the Emerald Vista Trail junction.
4.0 The footpath leads left (north) down to Moro Canyon.
4.3 Reach the bottom of Moro Canyon.
4.7 Return to the parking area.

East Cut-Across to Moro Ridge Loop

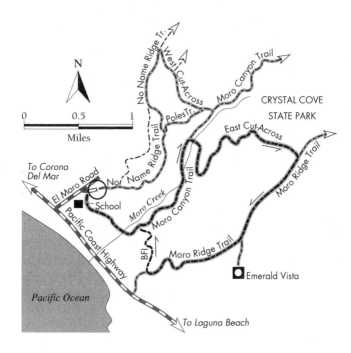

The hike: This hike takes you in a loop from the lower portions of Moro Canyon up to the high ridgeline on its southern edge, then back down to your starting point. A broad spectrum of terrain and habitat are explored without committing too much time, which the longer hikes in Crystal Cove State Park typically require. Spring will find the canyon bottom flowing with water and the hills green with fresh growth and seasonal wildflowers. As you descend the high Moro Ridge, you will be rewarded with spectacular ocean vistas. You will also be afforded views south and east into the wild canyons and hills that are now part of Laguna Coast Wilderness Park and Irvine Company Open Space.

To begin the hike, take the trail that heads south from the vicinity of the entrance booth and behind (east of) the trailer park. The trail winds downhill into the bottom of Moro Canyon at 0.4 mile.

Follow the Moro Canyon Trail left (east) up the canyon, and observe the open coastal sage scrub and grass hillsides. After a stream crossing, the trail climbs up onto the left (north) side of the creek. At 1.5 miles, you will come to the intersection with the East Cut-Across Trail, which is on your right (south).

Turn right, crossing the creek, and follow the East Cut-Across Trail for one mile as it winds up the canyon wall. At 2.5 miles, reach the intersection with the Moro Ridge Trail. Head right (west) on the Moro Ridge Trail as it gently descends along the ridgetop. Just before the trail begins a steep descent at 3.2 miles, a left-hand fork leads to the Emerald Vista. A detour to the Emerald Vista will add about 0.5 mile to your hike.

Continue down the Moro Ridge Trail until you are near the Pacific Coast Highway and the route becomes paved. Here, at 4 miles, you turn right onto the BFI footpath that heads down to the bottom of Moro Canyon. Once you reach the floor of Moro Canyon at 4.3 miles, turn left and retrace your steps back to the parking lot (4.7 miles).

Laurel Canyon–Bommer Ridge Loop

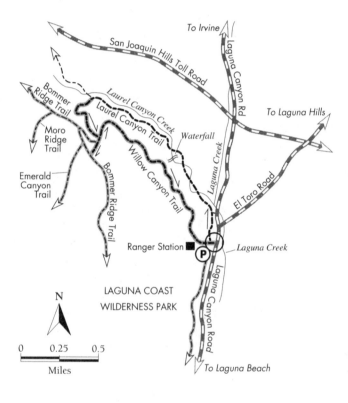

To Irvine

San Joaquin Hills Toll Road

Laguna Canyon Rd

To Laguna Hills

Bommer Ridge Trail

Laurel Canyon Creek

Laurel Canyon Trail

Waterfall

Laguna Creek

Moro Ridge Trail

Willow Canyon Trail

Emerald Canyon Trail

El Toro Road

Bommer Ridge Trail

Ranger Station

P

Laguna Creek

Laguna Canyon Road

N

LAGUNA COAST
WILDERNESS PARK

0   0.25   0.5

Miles

To Laguna Beach

2 0

5
LAUREL CANYON–BOMMER RIDGE LOOP

Type of hike: Loop.
Total distance: 3.5 miles.
Elevation gain: 665 feet.
Topo map: USGS Laguna Beach.
Jurisdiction: Laguna Coast Wilderness Park.
Finding the trailhead: From Interstate 5 (the Santa Ana Freeway) or Interstate 405 (the San Diego Freeway), take Laguna Canyon Road (California 133) southwest to a point just south of the intersection with El Toro Road. The park entrance is located on your right (west). Park volunteers and/or rangers will permit entry on dates of scheduled hikes only.

Key points:
0.3 Pass sandstone outcrops.
0.5 Make the first stream crossing.
0.8 Reach Laurel Canyon Falls.
1.5 Join the fire road and head left (southwest).
2.0 Reach the crest of the ridge.
3.5 Return to the parking area.

The hike: At the time of this writing, all access to, and hiking in, Laguna Coast Wilderness Park is restricted to docent-led tours. These hikes are informative and perfect family outings. (Note: Children must be able to complete the entire hike on their own.)

As you work your way up the secluded recesses of Laurel Canyon, you will have a chance to view scenery seen by few people. A large number of native plants, birds of prey, and migratory songbirds will be seen. In winter and spring, a variety of wildflowers sprout forth. The only sad note to this hike is the terrible intrusion of the San Joaquin Hills Toll Road through the upper reaches of the canyon.

There are plans to continue to acquire public ownership of much of the San Joaquin Hills adjacent to this park and Crystal Cove State Park. Once this is accomplished, greatly expanded and open access for hiking, mountain bicycling, and horseback riding should be available.

Hikes are conducted every Saturday and begin between 8 and 9 A.M. No dogs are allowed and there is a $2 fee. Consider making a much more generous donation. Call the Laguna Coast Wilderness Park at (714) 854-7108 to confirm times and dates.

The hike begins from the parking lot. Proceed left (north), up and over a small ridge into the open area of Laurel Canyon. Head up the footpath into the mouth of the canyon, passing old orchards and large sandstone outcrops at 0.3 mile.

The trail becomes shaded, and at 0.5 mile you make the first of three crossings of the seasonal Laurel Canyon Creek. At the second stream crossing, note the fine shell fossils in the creek. The trail begins to climb along the right side of the canyon until, at 0.8 mile, you reach a level spot and a last stream crossing atop the 50-foot Laurel Canyon Falls.

Wander along under ancient oak and sycamore trees as the canyon widens, until the footpath joins a narrow fire road at 1.5 miles. Here, you turn left (southwest) and follow the trail as it climbs upward out of the canyon to a trail junction. Head right (northwest) from the junction, and continue up a few hundred yards to the ridgeline at 2 miles, where you can enjoy views west to the Pacific Ocean and into Emerald Canyon.

Retrace your route downhill, but continue past the junction with the trail leading into Laurel Canyon. Continue downhill on the wide Willow Canyon Trail, which passes high above the southern side of Laurel Canyon. This trail leads you to the ranger station and your car at 3.5 miles.

West Ridge, Lynx, and Cholla Trails

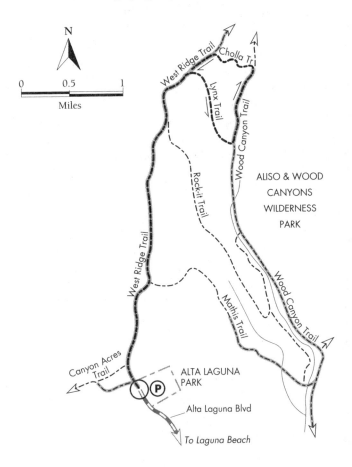

6
WEST RIDGE, LYNX, AND CHOLLA TRAILS

Type of hike: Loop.
Total distance: 5.3 miles.
Elevation gain: 640 feet.
Topo maps: USGS Laguna Beach and San Juan Capistrano.
Jurisdiction: Aliso & Wood Canyons Wilderness Park.
Finding the trailhead: From Interstate 5 (the Santa Ana Freeway) or Interstate 405 (the San Diego Freeway), take Laguna Canyon Road (California 133) southwest to Forest Avenue/Third Street. Take Third Street up the short, very steep hill. At the stop sign, turn left onto Park Avenue. Follow Park Avenue uphill to its end at Alta Laguna Boulevard. Turn left (north) onto Alta Laguna and go 0.2 mile to the parking area at Alta Laguna Park. The trail begins at the northwest corner of the parking area.

Key points:
0.5 Reach the junction with the Mathis Trail and stay left (north).
1.5 Arrive at the Rock-it Trail junction and stay left (north).
2.0 Turn right (east) onto Lynx Trail.
2.6 Reach the bottom of the canyon and turn left (north).
2.8 Turn left (northwest) at the Cholla Trail junction.
3.2 Rejoin the West Ridge Trail.
4.7 Arrive at the parking area.

The hike: This hike has it all, including vistas of the Pacific Ocean from the heights above Laguna Beach, and a visit to the depths of a coastal canyon shaded by ancient oaks and sycamores. Starting atop Alta Laguna Boulevard, you descend to the north along the West Ridge Trail as it undulates along the ridge separating busy Laguna Canyon from the quiet solitude of Wood Canyon. Eventually, the footpath takes you from the ridge into the upper reaches of Wood Canyon. During much of the year water flows in Wood Canyon Creek, and the careful observer will be rewarded with glimpses of wildlife. By returning to the West Ridge Trail via the Cholla Trail, you complete a loop and explore a variety of terrain.

From the parking area, head northwest on a path that soon joins the wide West Ridge Trail at the highest spot in Aliso & Wood Canyons Wilderness Park. Head north on the trail, which soon begins a long descent, then curves up slightly to the right (southeast). Stay left (north) at the junction with the Mathis Trail at 0.5 mile.

Another descent and a few small rises bring you to a junction with the Rock-it Trail near a water tank at 1.5 miles; stay left (north) here. Continue along the West Ridge Trail; a final descent brings you to a gate and another trail junction at 2 miles. Head right on the Lynx Trail, a wide footpath that rapidly descends the side of a sage scrub–covered ridge to the tree-shaded bottom of Wood Canyon at 2.6 miles.

The Lynx Trail deposits you on the wide Wood Canyon Trail, amid large oaks and next to Wood Canyon Creek. Head left (north), up the Wood Canyon Trail, until you reach an open area just before a park gate. From the left (northwest) side of the open area, proceed up the Cholla Trail (2.8 miles). This footpath climbs back up to meet the West Ridge Trail at 3.2 miles. Turn left (southwest) on the West Ridge Trail; you soon pass the Lynx Trail junction.

Continue the way you came, climbing steadily back to your car and starting point at 4.7 miles.

7
VALIDO TRAIL

Type of hike: Out-and-back.
Total distance: 2 miles.
Elevation gain: 400 feet.
Topo map: USGS San Juan Capistrano.
Jurisdiction: Aliso & Wood Canyons Wilderness Park.
Finding the trailhead: From Interstate 5 (the Santa Ana Freeway) or Interstate 405 (the San Diego Freeway), take Laguna Canyon Road (California 133) southwest to the Pacific Coast Highway (PCH/California 1). Head left (south) on the PCH for about 3.5 miles to West Street in South Laguna. Turn left (east) onto West Street, go less than 0.2 mile, and make a left-hand (north) turn onto Valido Drive. As you round the curve, the trailhead is on your left (north). Park on the street, but avoid blocking any residential access.

Key points:
1.0 Reach the crest of Aliso Peak.

The hike: Looking for a short, family-oriented hike that leads to a stunning ocean vista? This hike may be for you. Though the Valido Trail makes a significant climb from a residential area in South Laguna, the trail is short enough that even small children can be coaxed along.

The hike finishes atop a rounded summit that hangs above Aliso Creek and the Pacific Ocean. The surrounding

Valido Trail

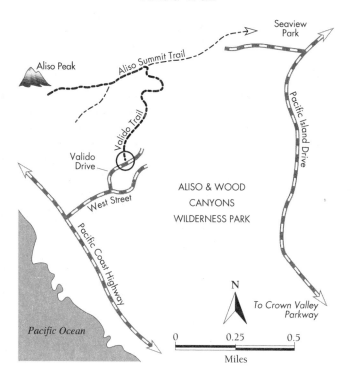

terrain is precipitously steep in places, so it is important that you don't wander off the established trails. Though the wild upper Valido Canyon is somewhat marred by development atop the ridge, the trail heads through largely unspoiled open space. Once atop the summit, you are rewarded with spectacular views west to the Pacific Ocean, and northeast up Aliso Canyon into the heart of Aliso & Wood Canyons Wilderness Park.

From the gate at the trailhead, head up the canyon on the wide Valido Trail until a sign marks the point where the trail becomes a footpath. The trail proceeds along a small creek for a short distance before making a steep climb up a hillside. Log steps and switchbacks make the short, but steep, ascent fairly straightforward. At the second switchback, you can gaze west to the Pacific Ocean and east up the narrow canyon.

The route's grade slackens as you continue up to the ridge, where the trail intersects with another wide trail. Turn left (west) on the Aliso Summit Trail at the trail junction and go straight west, eventually making a short, but steep, climb up to the summit of Aliso Peak. This is the turnaround point. Take time to enjoy the view before heading back to the car on the same path.

The Foothills

The foothills of Orange County provide a wide diversity of geography and wildlife. For many years, much of the open space in Orange County has been closed to public access, with cattle grazing and agriculture the prevalent land use. Though large landowners and their "appointed" representatives on the Orange County Board of Supervisors have pushed hard for development of most of rural Orange County, notable efforts have been made to preserve a portion of these unique and valuable habitats.

A number of open space, state, and county parks have saved pieces of this landscape from the blade of the developer's bulldozer, though more land remains threatened. Canyons, grasslands, lakes, seasonal streams, and hilltops are all found here. The hikes in this section range from short strolls along strips of open space near developments to more remote locales where you can almost imagine the Orange County of 50 or even 100 years past.

8
TELEGRAPH CANYON TRAIL
VIA RIMCREST ENTRANCE

Type of hike: Out-and-back.
Total distance: 4.8 miles.
Elevation gain: 525 feet.
Topo maps: USGS Yorba Linda and Prado Dam.
Jurisdiction: Chino Hills State Park.
Finding the trailhead: Take California 91 (the Riverside Freeway) east to Imperial Highway (California 90) and head north. Follow Imperial Highway to Yorba Linda Boulevard, and turn east (right). At Fairmont Boulevard, turn left (north). After 1.8 miles turn left onto Rimcrest Street. Park on the right-hand side of Rimcrest Street near Blue Gum. Parking is permitted from 8 A.M. until dark. The trailhead lies straight ahead at the end of Rimcrest Street.

Key points:
0.4 The footpath reaches the bottom of Telegraph Canyon; turn right (east) on the Telegraph Canyon Trail.
2.4 Arrive at the shaded picnic area.

The hike: Telegraph Canyon runs eastward from its mouth at the Carbon Canyon up toward one of Chino Hills' highest points, San Juan Peak. Along the way, a rich riparian habitat is encountered. The upper section of this large canyon offers many cool spots in the shade of ancient oak and sy-

Telegraph Canyon Trail via Rimcrest Entrance

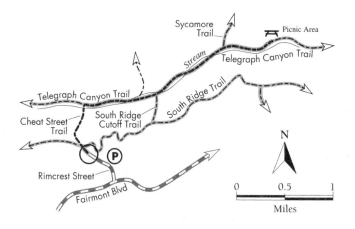

camore trees. The surrounding hills hide all evidence of human development, providing a sense of remoteness seldom encountered in congested Orange County. During winter months, the emerald green hillsides and free-flowing creek are delightful. By using the Rimcrest entrance, you are plunged immediately into the upper reaches of Telegraph Canyon.

To begin, pass the metal gate at the park entrance and proceed more or less due north on the Cheat Street Trail, across the fire road (the South Ridge Trail). The trail begins a descent into a narrow side canyon, staying on its left side.

Eventually, it crosses a stream, and terminates on the wide Telegraph Canyon Trail at 0.4 mile. Note this trail junction for your return.

You are now in the depths of Telegraph Canyon. Turn right (east) and proceed up the trail along the canyon bottom. After the occasional seasonal stream crossing, you will see trails that head both left and right, up side canyons and hillsides. Don't stray from the canyon bottom.

Telegraph Canyon Trail begins to pass under an increasing number of sycamores and oaks, while paralleling the stream. The grade increases slightly, and the Sycamore Trail heads off to the left (north). Stay on the main trail along the canyon bottom; soon you will reach a nicely shaded section of trail, with a beautiful clearing on the right (south). A picnic table is under the oaks at 2.4 miles, and is a perfect place for lunch or a snack.

After resting and relaxing, simply return the way you came, making sure to take the footpath on your left back up to the Rimcrest entrance and your car.

9
WEIR CANYON TRAIL LOOP

Type of hike: Loop.
Total distance: 4 miles.
Elevation gain: 600 feet.
Topo map: USGS Black Star Canyon.
Jurisdiction: Weir Canyon Regional Park.
Finding the trailhead: Take California 91 (the Riverside Freeway) east to the Weir Canyon exit and head south. Turn right (west) at Serrano Avenue. Follow Serrano Avenue until you reach Hidden Canyon Road. Turn left (south) onto Hidden Canyon Road and follow it until you reach the dead end at Overlook Terrace. Park at the corner by the barrier. *Do not park* in the residential areas or along Avenida de Santiago.

Key points:
0.1 Turn left at the gate, following the footpath.
0.3 Another path joins from the left; stay right (northeast).
0.4 Cross the small stream.
2.5 The trail curves left next to a housing development.
3.5 Reach the cul-de-sac; head down Avenida de Santiago.
3.8 Turn left (south) on Hidden Canyon Road to your car.

The hike: Weir Canyon is one of the newest and least known of the Orange County regional parks, a small jewel amidst the increased development of the Anaheim Hills region. The

Weir Canyon Trail Loop

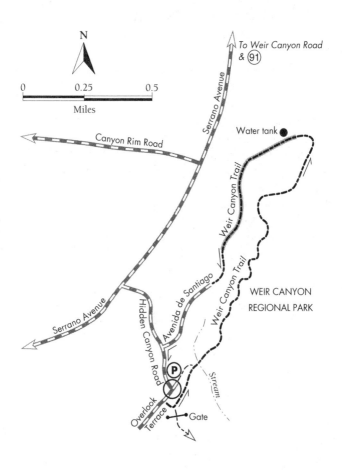

N

0   0.25   0.5
Miles

To Weir Canyon Road & (91)

Serrano Avenue

Canyon Rim Road

Water tank ●

Weir Canyon Trail

Weir Canyon Trail

Avenida de Santiago

Serrano Avenue

Hidden Canyon Road

WEIR CANYON
REGIONAL PARK

Stream

P

Overlook Terrace

Gate

current park is a relatively small sliver of land, but it is slated to be expanded eastward to the Eastern Foothill Toll Road, which will more than triple its size.

As you follow this trail, you are afforded excellent views eastward into serene valleys and rugged foothills, and toward the higher reaches of the Santa Ana Mountains. The trail winds in and out of small side canyons on the western edge of Weir Canyon.

From your car, take the wide trail/fire road directly east and slightly downhill. At 0.1 mile, you will come to a gate. Turn left uphill on an unmarked but obvious foot trail.

The path gradually rises and levels, with scenic overlooks into Weir Canyon on your right (southeast) and sandstone outcrops to your left (northwest). At an open spot at 0.3 mile, just before the trail descends under oaks, a trail intersects from the left. Stay right, descending to a seasonal stream crossing at 0.4 mile.

From the stream, the trail alternately climbs and descends while at the same time winding in and out of small side canyons. Pass a small gray sandstone bluff directly above the trail, which then heads slightly west, passing over a ridge.

The trail continues along the upper reaches of Weir Canyon, bordering a residential development at 2.5 miles. At this point, the trail begins to head in a southerly direction, passing a large water tank. Follow the trail along the ridge, then down to the end of Avenida de Santiago at 3.5 miles. An easy downhill walk on Avenida de Santiago, then a left onto Hidden Canyon Road at 3.8 miles, leads back to your car.

10
SANTIAGO CREEK TRAIL LOOP

Type of hike: Loop.
Total distance: 2.2 miles.
Elevation gain: 100 feet.
Topo map: USGS Orange.
Jurisdiction: Santiago Oaks Regional Park.
Finding the trailhead: From California 55 (the Newport Freeway), take the Katella Avenue exit and head east on Katella Avenue. Turn left (north) at Windes Drive. The park sign can be easy to miss. Follow Windes Drive to the park gate.

Key points:
0.5 Reach the picnic area.
1.0 The dam comes into view.
1.7 Arrive at the Wilderness Loop Trail junction.

The hike: Santiago Oaks Regional Park rests on a portion of the old Rancho Santiago de Santa Ana, which was granted to Jose Yorba by the Spanish governor Arillaga in 1810. In the late 1800s, this area was prowled by several notorious bandits, including Joaquin Murietta and Three-Fingered Jack. The outlaws would sweep down from the hills and terrorize local communities or rob the Butterfield Stage, which passed through the lower Santiago Canyon area.

Santiago Creek Trail Loop

Overlook

Bobcat

Picnic Area

Santiago Creek Trail

Santiago Creek

Oak Trail

Oak Trail

Wilderness Loop Trail

Rinker Grove Trail

Rinker Grove Trail

Santiago Creek Trail

Dam

Historic Dam Trail

Santiago Creek

SANTIAGO OAKS
REGIONAL PARK

P

Windes Drive

Santiago Creek

N

0   0.1   0.2

Miles

Santiago Oaks Regional Park is open daily from 7 A.M. to sunset. Entrance fees are $2 on weekdays and $4 on weekends. Rangers are not always on duty, so bring either quarters or very crisp dollar bills.

From the far end of the parking lot, follow the paved trail east past the information sign to a dirt trail, where you turn right. The trail forks at another large sign. Continue straight on the Santiago Creek Trail, which proceeds uphill.

Continue straight past junctions with Sourgrass and Historic Dam Trails when the trail levels. You will soon arrive atop the remnants of a dam originally constructed in 1879.

From here, the trail descends slightly, passing a picnic area at 0.5 mile, and eventually reaches a junction with the Oak and Rinker Grove Trails. Continue straight ahead. The trail meanders a bit, eventually reaching a stream crossing (after winter rains, the creek level may preclude a crossing). The trail proceeds through a narrow, water-carved corridor that is covered with lush vines, then heads uphill to where railroad-tie steps lead to a view of Villa Park Dam at the 1-mile mark.

Reverse your course to the picnic area and head right onto the Oak Trail, which heads uphill to the right (north). Pass through an open grassy meadow and the wooden fence. At 1.7 miles, turn left (west) onto the Wilderness Loop Trail. Follow this trail along rolling terrain past several trail junctions, eventually reaching a concrete bridge and a three-way trail intersection. Head right, and take the trail that meanders back west, crossing the creek and climbing up railroad ties, to the paved road. Head left along the side of the road to get back to your car.

11
PETERS CANYON LAKE LOOP

Type of hike: Loop.
Total distance: 2.5 miles.
Elevation gain: 250 feet.
Topo map: USGS Orange.
Jurisdiction: Peters Canyon Regional Park.
Finding the trailhead: From California 55 (the Newport Freeway), take the Chapman Avenue exit and head east on Chapman Avenue to Jamboree Boulevard. Turn right (south) onto Jamboree Boulevard; after 0.6 mile, turn right onto Canyon View Lane. From Interstate 5 (the Santa Ana Freeway), take Jamboree Boulevard north for 5.3 miles. Turn left onto Canyon View Lane. The parking area and park entrance are on your left. A fee is required.

Key points:
0.2 Reach the corner of Jamboree Boulevard.
0.5 Arrive at the Peters Canyon Trail junction.
0.6 Turn right (west) below the dam.
1.1 Reach a bench overlooking the reservoir.
1.3 At the Lake View Trail junction, turn right (north).
1.8 Turn right and follow the lakeshore.

The hike: The sage-covered hills east of Tustin and Orange look out upon the foothills of the Santa Ana Mountains, and despite the encroaching development, you can still get

41

Peters Canyon Lake Loop

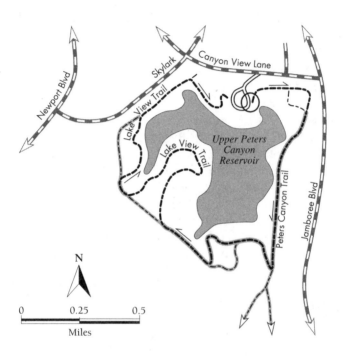

a taste of old Orange County. This trail circles the 55-acre Upper Peters Canyon Reservoir, which provides valuable habitat to migrating waterfowl. The rolling terrain takes you from marsh edge to open hillsides looking east over the lake toward the crest of the northern Santa Ana Mountains. This area originally was part of the Spanish Rancho Lomas de

Santiago. Later, as part of the Irvine Ranch, it was leased out to various farmers. One of these early farmers was James Peters, for whom the canyon is named.

Walk east from the parking lot, turning left on the trail located just before the picnic tables. Turn right on a footpath under the trees or, if it is wet, continue to the corner of Canyon View Avenue and Jamboree Boulevard at 0.2 mile, and turn right (south).

Reach a fire road and turn right, up a short hill, to Peters Canyon Trail at 0.5 mile. Turn right again, and head down. At the bottom of the hill (0.6 mile), turn right below the dam, then take the right fork up the short, steep hill that sits above the dam. There is a bench at the top of the hill at 1.1 miles.

Turn right and follow the road down, and then up again. Turn right onto the Lake View Trail at 1.3 miles, just beyond the crest of the hill. The Lake View Trail heads mostly downhill toward, and then along, the lakeshore at 1.8 miles, passing another bench along the way.

Eventually, you will turn right onto a wide path/road. Follow the road as it skirts the lake, then turn right onto a narrowing path. The path runs in and out of brush along the northern shoreline of the reservoir, eventually leading you back to the parking lot.

12
BORREGO CANYON TO RED ROCK CANYON

Type of hike: Out-and-back.
Total distance: 5 miles.
Elevation gain: 460 feet.
Topo map: USGS El Toro.
Jurisdiction: Whiting Ranch Wilderness Park.
Finding the trailhead: From Interstate 5 (the Santa Ana Freeway), take the El Toro Road exit and go east 4.7 miles to Portola Parkway. Turn left (north) onto Portola Parkway and drive 1.8 miles to the signal at Market. Turn right, then make an immediate left, where you will find parking for Whiting Ranch Wilderness Park. The entrance and trailhead are located in the northern end of the Foothill Ranch Marketplace shopping center.

Key points:
1.6 Turn right at the junction with Mustard Road.
1.8 Turn left onto the Red Rock Canyon Trail.
2.5 Reach the end of the trail and the turnaround point.

The hike: The trailhead and entrance to Whiting Ranch will not inspire you. It literally is located in a shopping center parking lot. Do not despair. As soon as you descend into Borrego Canyon, the sycamore-shaded trail spirits you far from signs of intrusion. The trail follows beside, across, and

Borrego Canyon to Red Rock Canyon

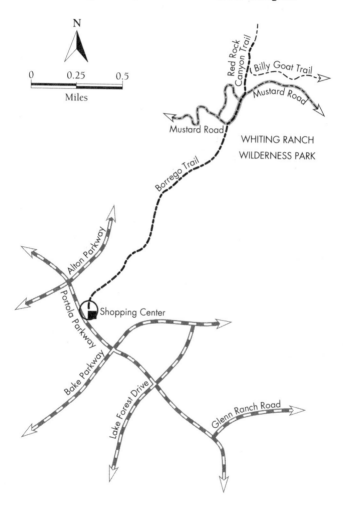

through Borrego Canyon Creek, and reaches the more open and undeveloped hillsides. Eventually, you strike out onto the narrow and very scenic Red Rock Canyon Trail, which meanders through oak woodland and coastal sage scrub to 100-foot-high red sandstone cliffs in Red Rock Canyon. These striking rocks have been shaped by water and wind erosion.

From the trailhead, head downhill about 25 yards until you intersect the Borrego Trail, and bear right (northeast). The wide trail gradually gains elevation. As you continue up the canyon, the trail becomes a narrower footpath and makes several stream crossings. A small footbridge traverses a section of steeper wash.

The trail stays in the shady canyon bottom under oaks and sycamores. The footpath merges with the wide Mustard Road at 1.6 miles. Turn right (east) and walk uphill, passing one trail, until you reach a small wooden footbridge on the left. This is the start of the Red Rock Canyon Trail (1.8 miles).

Cross the bridge and head north through the more open coastal scrub sage and oak woodland along the canyon. You soon reach the upper portions of the canyon, where telltale red sandstone cliffs rise around you. The trail ends near the top of the canyon at 2.5 miles.

Return to your car the way you came.

13
LIVE OAK TRAIL

Type of hike: Out-and-back.
Total distance: 3 miles.
Elevation gain: 600 feet.
Topo map: USGS Santiago Peak.
Jurisdiction: O'Neill Regional Park.
Finding the trailhead: From Interstate 5 (the Santa Ana Freeway), take El Toro Road east for 7 miles and make a left-hand (east) turn at the signal at Valley Vista. Proceed up Valley Vista a short distance to Meadow Ridge, and make a right (south) turn. Follow Meadow Ridge to its end. Parking is available in a small lot at the end of the street, or along the west side of Meadow Ridge.

Key points:
0.4 Cross the footbridge and turn right (uphill/east).
1.0 Make a sharp right turn (uphill/south).
1.3 Take the left fork to the summit.
1.5 Enjoy the view from the top.

The hike: This section of the Live Oak Trail, which runs farther north toward Whiting Ranch Wilderness Park, is a combination of narrow foot trail and fire road in the western section of O'Neill Park. This hike traverses some of the less traveled and most scenic areas of O'Neill Park. Despite the trailhead's proximity to residential development, within

Live Oak Trail

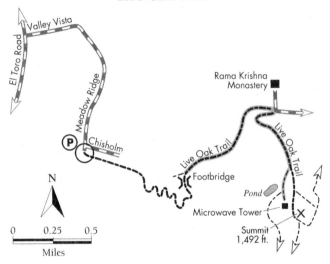

minutes from your car you will find yourself in open woodland and grassy meadows. Over the course of 1.5 miles, you climb 600 feet to a spectacular summit and observation point. Picnic tables, an interpretive plaque, and a good view in all directions await. Unfortunately, the view south into Rancho Santa Margarita portends the future of most of southern Orange County—a homogenous sea of development.

From the car, head straight south and then turn left (east) down a paved service road that provides access to a nursery. Continue straight (east) until you are on a dirt trail that proceeds behind residences, then breaks out toward the hills.

Hike up the short, steep, and winding trail through thick woodland plants. Drop down the other side of the ridge, through an oak-surrounded meadow and across a small bridge at 0.4 mile. Beyond the bridge, turn right (east) onto a fire road. Proceed up the fire road to a trail intersection at 1 mile. The Rama Krishna Monastery is on the hill to your left.

Make a severe right-hand turn at the intersection, and proceed up the fire road to where it levels and another road splits off to your left at 1.3 miles. Take the left-hand road, which narrows and heads up a steep incline to the high point (1,492 feet) at the top of the hill (1.5 miles). There are picnic tables and a plaque describing the 360-degree view that runs from Saddleback in the northeast to the San Joaquin Hills in the west. Retrace the route back to your car.

14
WAGON WHEEL PARK LOOP

Type of hike: Loop.
Total distance: 2.7 miles.
Elevation gain: 450 feet.
Topo map: USGS Cañada Gobernadora.
Jurisdiction: Wagon Wheel Wilderness Park (a.k.a. General Thomas F. Riley Wilderness Park).
Finding the trailhead: From Interstate 5 (the Santa Ana Freeway), take the Oso Parkway exit and drive east on Oso Parkway for 6 miles. The park entrance (a right-hand turn) lies 50 yards before the stop sign at Oso Parkway and Coto De Caza Drive. A short dirt road (0.2 mile) leads to the parking area and ranger station. There is a $2 per vehicle fee. A toilet and bulletin board are the only facilities available. No camping or water is to be found in the park.

Key points:
0.3 Stay right at the Sycamore Loop turnoff.
0.7 Reach the junction of the Horned Toad Trail.
1.0 Rejoin the Oak Canyon Trail and turn left (north).
1.5 Reach Vista Ridge and Mule Deer trail intersections.
1.9 Turn left (north) onto Pheasant Run Trail.
2.3 Turn right (south) onto Wagon Wheel Trail.

Wagon Wheel Park Loop

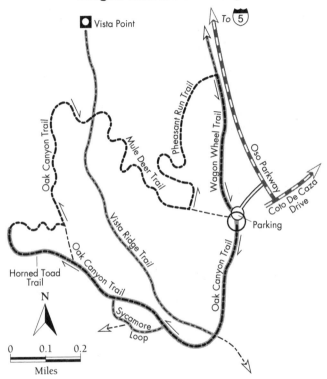

The hike: Wagon Wheel Wilderness Park is a spare 475 acres of rolling sage-covered hills and oak- and sycamore-shaded valleys. It was officially opened in 1994 and renamed for a former Orange County supervisor, General Thomas F. Riley, to commemorate his retirement.

The park has a host of pleasant and usually uncrowded trails. This hike circumnavigates most of the park and takes you on a tour of the best trails. You will climb up and down in this rolling landscape, amid ancient oaks in the low valleys, and atop grassy hilltops. Many people hope that more of the beautiful surrounding hills and valleys will be preserved and added to this small park. Barring this, Wagon Wheel may become only a curious anomaly in an otherwise barren landscape of ubiquitous development.

From the parking area, head south past the bulletin board on the Oak Canyon Trail. Soon, the Vista Ridge Trail heads up right (northwest), and an unnamed fire road heads left. Continue straight ahead, passing the Sycamore Loop turnoff on your left (south) at 0.3 mile.

The Oak Canyon Trail takes a right-hand turn under the oaks; head straight (west) on Horned Toad Trail at 0.7 mile, walking up the hill. At the top of the hill, you will enjoy good views of most of the park. Continue on the Horned Toad Trail as it turns right (east) and winds back down to Oak Canyon Trail at 1 mile.

Turn left (north), following Oak Canyon Trail past a pond. Cross a creek and ascend to the Vista Ridge Trail fire road at 1.5 miles. Directly across the fire road is the top of Mule Deer Trail, a narrow footpath. Follow this down into a small valley to a junction with the Pheasant Run Trail, which heads uphill on your left (north) at 1.9 miles. Take the enjoyable Pheasant Run Trail over a low hill, then back down to where it ends at the Wagon Wheel Trail.

Turn right (south) onto Wagon Wheel Trail at 2.3 miles. It heads under the shade of old oak trees back to the trailhead.

15
WEST RIDGE AND
OAK TRAIL LOOP

Type of hike: Loop.
Total distance: 3.4 miles.
Elevation gain: 360 feet.
Topo map: USGS Cañada Gobernadora.
Jurisdiction: Caspers Wilderness Park.
Finding the trailhead: From Interstate 5 (the Santa Ana Freeway), take the Ortega Highway (California 74) east for 7.6 miles. The park entrance is on your left (north). The Dick Loskorn Trailhead is found by driving north past the park entrance and visitor center to the end of the paved road, and turning left at the windmills. The trail is marked "Nature Trail," and begins on the west side of the parking area.

Key points:
0.1 Head left (northwest) on the Dick Loskorn Trail.
0.8 Reach the West Ridge Trail and turn right (north).
1.6 Descend the Star Rise Trail.
2.3 Reach the Oak Trail junction and go right (south).

The hike: Though not a long hike, the varied terrain, excellent vistas, and general lack of traffic make this one of the premier hikes in Caspers Wilderness Park. However, summer in Caspers Park, particularly on the exposed ridges tra-

West Ridge and Oak Trail Loop

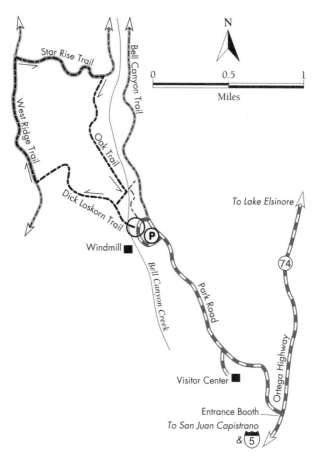

Star Rise Trail

Bell Canyon Trail

West Ridge Trail

Oak Trail

N

0   0.5   1

Miles

Dick Loskorn Trail

P

Windmill ■

Bell Canyon Creek

To Lake Elsinore

74

Park Road

Ortega Highway

Visitor Center ■

Entrance Booth

To San Juan Capistrano

& 5

versed on this hike, can be unpleasant and enervating. Fall, winter, or spring are ideal for hiking here.

The beginning and end of this hike pass under tall sycamores and ancient oak trees. The initial climb up to the West Ridge on the Dick Loskorn Trail winds up a ridge of soft, exposed sandstone cliffs. Care should be taken here. Once the wide West Ridge Trail is reached, you hike the high ridge north, with unsurpassed views east and west. The descent back into Bell Canyon takes you on a quiet footpath that leads back to your starting point.

From the Nature Trail sign, head northwest across the Bell Canyon creekbed into the oak woods, passing a park bench. At 0.1 mile, you will turn left at the junction with the Dick Loskorn Trail. Head west under the trees, then break out onto a sandstone ridge, which can be quite narrow in places.

After a continuous climb, you reach the West Ridge Trail fire road at 0.8 mile. Follow the West Ridge Trail right (north). Enjoy good views east into Bell Canyon, and west into the still undeveloped Cañada Gobernadora.

After traveling about 0.8 mile north on the West Ridge Trail, you will reach and turn right (east) onto Star Rise Trail (1.6 miles). Star Rise Trail, a fire road, descends at a gradual incline east into Bell Canyon. After reaching the canyon bottom at 2.3 miles, turn right (south) onto the Oak Trail.

The Oak Trail is a lightly traveled footpath under oaks and sycamores that roughly parallels the Bell Canyon creekbed and returns you to the Dick Loskorn Trail junction. From here, retrace your route back to your car.

The Mountains

The Santa Ana Mountains are a dominant backdrop for Orange County, scenically, geographically, and historically. The two highest peaks, Santiago and Modjeska, form the distinctive "Old Saddleback," whose silhouette can be seen from throughout the county. These high peaks, and most of the Santa Ana high country, lie within the confines of the Cleveland National Forest. A wide variety of footpaths, fire roads, and paved roads crisscross the range and abundant hiking opportunities exist here. Wildlife is also varied. The Santa Anas are seasonal or permanent home to hundreds of bird species; dozens of mammal, reptile, and amphibian species; and seven species of fish. Mountain lions are found in many areas.

The Santa Ana Mountains can be quite rugged, with high ridges and deep canyons. Due to the density of coastal chaparral, travel off established trails can be extremely difficult. At 5,687 feet, the highest point, Santiago Peak, is not particularly lofty. However, the weather high above the coastal plains can be both extremely warm and extremely cold. These mountains are not to be taken lightly.

Much of the Santa Ana range lies within the Cleveland National Forest. Due to congressional efforts to de-fund the USDA Forest Service's recreation budget, parking in day use parking areas requires the purchase and display of a Forest Adventure Pass. Day use or annual passes can be purchased at USDA Forest Service offices and most outdoor stores.

16
SILVERADO CANYON–
SILVERADO MOTORWAY

Type of hike: Out-and-back.
Total distance: 4.5 miles.
Elevation gain: 520 feet.
Topo maps: USGS Santiago Peak and Corona South.
Jurisdiction: Cleveland National Forest.
Permits: A Forest Adventure Pass is required.
Finding the trailhead: From California 55 (the Newport Freeway), take Chapman Avenue east to Jamboree Boulevard. Proceed straight; Chapman becomes Santiago Canyon Road. Drive 6.7 miles southeast on Santiago Canyon Road and turn left onto Silverado Canyon Road. Follow Silverado Canyon Road east for 5.4 miles to a parking area and USDA Forest Service gate. From Interstate 5 (the Santa Ana Freeway), go east 13.6 miles on El Toro Road/Santiago Canyon Road). At Silverado Canyon Road, turn right (east). Follow Silverado Canyon Road for 5.4 miles to the parking area.

Key points:
0.1 Take the footpath on the left.
2.2 Reach a large flat area with excellent views to the west.

The hike: Today, the Silverado Motorway is a footpath that makes broad switchbacks up the sage and chaparral-covered

Silverado Canyon—Silverado Motorway

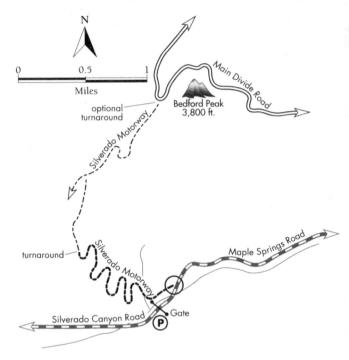

canyon wall toward Bedford Peak. Once a fire road, it has so deteriorated over the years that it is difficult to believe it was once passable by vehicles.

This hike on the motorway takes you from upper Silverado Canyon to a ridgetop view of the Pacific Ocean. Though the incline is never great, it is a steady climb up the canyon wall. The views into Silverado Canyon, toward Old Saddleback, and westward become grander the higher you climb. Eventually, you reach the crest of a high ridge separating Ladd and Silverado Canyons. A mile farther up the ridge trail lies the Main Divide Road, and a short distance farther, the summit of Bedford Peak, one of the higher summits in the Santa Ana Mountains. This hike is quite exposed and should be avoided in hot weather.

Begin at the USDA Forest Service gate and proceed up the Maple Springs (Silverado Canyon) Road until you reach a stream. Cross the stream and proceed up the canyon for approximately 100 yards. The Silverado Motorway footpath is on your left at 0.1 mile; go westward up this trail.

The trail cuts north up a side canyon. In winter, both this side canyon and the trail run with water. Cross the waterway, if in season, and begin your journey upward. The trail is eroded in places.

After several switchbacks, you reach a rocky flat where the trail cuts back east up toward the ridge. Continue up the trail as it proceeds east up the side of the ridge.

At 2.2 miles, you reach a large flat area on the ridgetop. Explore the views from various aspects of the ridge before heading back the way you came to the shady bottom of Silverado Canyon.

Option: If you feel energized, continue on the trail as it heads east along the ridge. At the 3.3-mile mark, you intersect Main Divide Road. Either return along the path you've already followed, or continue an extra 0.5 mile up and right (east) on Main Divide Road to Bedford Peak (3,800 feet).

17
SANTIAGO TRAIL

Type of hike: Out-and-back.
Total distance: 5 miles.
Elevation gain: 600 feet.
Topo maps: USGS El Toro and Santiago Peak.
Jurisdiction: Cleveland National Forest.
Permits: A Forest Adventure Pass is not required.
Finding the trailhead: From Interstate 5 (the Santa Ana Freeway), take El Toro Road (which becomes Santiago Canyon Road) eastward for approximately 8.9 miles and turn right at the Modjeska Grade Road turnoff. This right-hand turn is located about 1.3 miles past the Live Oak Canyon Road turnoff (also known as Cook's Corner). Park well off the road surface near the bottom of Modjeska Grade Road toward its junction with Santiago Canyon Road. No parking is permitted higher up the road.

Key points:
2.5 Reach the turnaround point.

The hike: The Santiago Trail is a former fire road that is being encouraged to revert to a nice foot trail. Though the Santiago Trail leads 8 miles to Old Camp in the upper reaches of Modjeska (Santiago) Canyon, this hike only proceeds up the first 2.5 miles. From the high turnaround point,

Santiago Trail

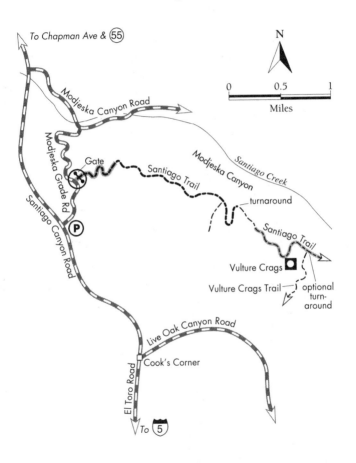

you will enjoy sweeping views out toward the San Joaquin Hills near Laguna Beach, and into the upper wild reaches of Modjeska Canyon.

The Vulture Crags are less than a mile beyond the turn-around point of this hike. These conglomerate cliffs were once a roosting place for the endangered California condor. Like the grizzly bear, also once a resident of the Santa Ana Mountains, the condor was laid low by rifle bullets and poison. Also, deep in the recesses of the upper Modjeska Canyon, evidence of mining activity from the 1870s can still be found.

From your car, proceed up Modjeska Grade Road to a point just below its crest. A steel gate and the trailhead are on your right. Respect any fire or other closure signs; if none are posted, go east, up the fire road as it runs along the side of the ridge. At a sharp left turn, you gain a good view to the southwest.

A short distance farther, the trail narrows and you get your first glimpse to the northeast into Modjeska Canyon. Stay on the main trail where various informal trails head up the steep ridge.

The main trail passes along the north side of the ridgeline, affording unobstructed views into Modjeska Canyon and toward the twin peaks of Old Saddleback. The trail gently descends a bit, then begins to climb a grade on the west side of the ridge. At the top of the incline, the trail levels, drops some, then rounds another bend. Stay left on the main trail where a footpath descends right.

Continue along the Santiago Trail. At 2.5 miles, about 150 yards past a sharp switchback, you will reach a level spot. At this spot, the end point of this hike, you may enjoy good views into the upper reaches of Modjeska Canyon. Return to your car the way you came.

Option: From the level turnaround spot, proceed up the Santiago Trail to a point where a long descent begins. After 0.6 mile, the trail rapidly descends to a level area along the ridge. Here, you can look west and see Vulture Crags, the conglomerate rock outcrop that was once the nesting site of California condors. Old mining trails are also found in this vicinity, as are old mineshafts, which can be seen below (to the east) in Modjeska Canyon. Return via the same route.

18
HOLY JIM FALLS TRAIL

Type of hike: Out-and-back.
Total distance: 2.7 miles.
Elevation gain: 620 feet.
Topo map: USGS Santiago Peak.
Jurisdiction: Cleveland National Forest.
Permits: A Forest Adventure Pass is required.
Finding the trailhead: From Interstate 5 (the Santa Ana Freeway), take El Toro Road east for 7.6 miles and turn right (east) onto Live Oak Canyon Road. Follow Live Oak Canyon Road south and east for 4.4 miles and make a left-hand (east) turn onto the dirt Trabuco Creek Road (6S13). Follow the bumpy dirt road east for 4.7 miles to the Holy Jim Canyon Road (6S14) turnoff. Park in the large flat area at the intersection of Trabuco Creek Road and Holy Jim Canyon Road. *Do not* drive up Holy Jim Canyon Road. Traffic is restricted to local residents.

Key points:
0.5 Reach the Holy Jim trailhead.
0.7 Pass the fig trees that are remnants of an old orchard.
1.1 The picnic rock is on the left.
1.4 Reach the waterfall and turnaround point.

The hike: Undoubtedly, the hike into Holy Jim Canyon is one of the most scenic and interesting in the Santa Ana

Holy Jim Falls Trail

Mountains. The hike passes under a multitude of trees, and crosses Holy Jim Creek many times before eventually reaching the falls, a 35-foot cascade and popular picnic spot.

The canyon is named for James T. Smith, a canyon resident and beekeeper during the late 1800s who was renowned for his foul language. Nicknamed variously "Cussin' Jim," "Lyin' Jim," "Greasy Jim," and "Salvation Jim," government mapmakers bestowed the sanitized "Holy Jim" on the canyon with which he was closely associated. The numerous fig trees found throughout the canyon are the wild descendants of Smith's fig orchard, which, along with his house, burned in a 1908 fire.

From the parking area, begin walking left (north) up Holy Jim Canyon Road (6S14) to the Holy Jim trailhead at 0.5 mile. The trail meanders up the canyon, alternating between shade and sun. After the second stream crossing, you may see a stone wall, the only remnants of Jim Smith's cabin. Poison oak is common on this route, so stay on the trail and be sure you are familiar with its identification.

Further along the trail, you can glimpse Santiago Peak far up the ridge to your left (north). Continue up the trail until you reach a clearing. Picnic Rock is on your left (west) at 1.1 mile, and the large oak to the right (east) is thought to be over 500 years old.

The trail soon makes a final stream crossing (to the west side of the canyon); a small stone "check dam" is found here. Once you cross to the opposite side of the creek, the trail splits. Take the right fork in the trail, and continue upstream; in spring and summer, swarms of ladybugs can be found along the trail. After 400 yards, the trail ends at the falls at 1.4 miles.

Head back the way you came, enjoying the scenery and gentle downhill grade as you return to your starting point.

Option: You may choose to complete a more challenging 10-mile hike that leads up toward the higher reaches of Old Saddleback. From the trail intersection 400 yards below the falls, take the left-hand fork. The trail quickly switchbacks up the steep western slope of Holy Jim Canyon. Eventually, the trail contours along the canyon wall and terminates at the Main Divide Road, some 2,000 vertical feet higher. Summer sun should be avoided; spring brings a number of bright wildflowers.

19
TRABUCO TRAIL

Type of hike: Out-and-back.
Total distance: 3.6 miles.
Elevation gain: 880 feet.
Topo map: USGS Alberhill.
Jurisdiction: Cleveland National Forest.
Permits: A Forest Adventure Pass is required.
Finding the trailhead: From Interstate 5 (the Santa Ana Freeway), take El Toro Road east for 7.6 miles, then turn right (east) onto Live Oak Canyon Road. Follow Live Oak Canyon Road south and east for 4.4 miles and make a left-hand (east) turn onto the Trabuco Creek dirt road (6S13). Follow the bumpy dirt road for 5.7 miles (past the Holy Jim Canyon turnoff) to its end at a USDA Forest Service gate. The trail starts here. Parking is limited. If no parking is available, park back at the large flat area at the intersection of Trabuco Creek Road and Holy Jim Canyon Road.

Key points:
0.9 Yeager Mesa lies on the right (south) side of the canyon.
1.8 Reach the Horsethief Trail junction.

The hike: Though the drive up the dirt Trabuco Creek Road to the trailhead can be bumpy—and is not advisable during a heavy runoff—the hiking in Holy Jim Canyon and the

Trabuco Trail

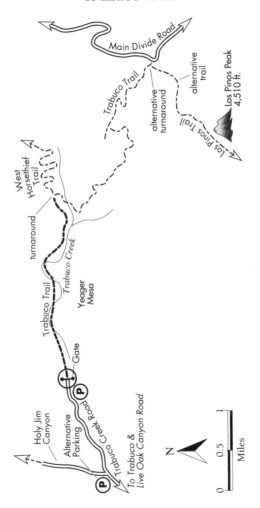

Holy Jim Canyon

Alternative Parking

Trabuco Creek Road

To Trabuco & Live Oak Canyon Road

Gate

Trabuco Trail

Yeager Mesa

Trabuco Creek

turnaround

West Horsethief Trail

Trabuco Trail

Main Divide Road

alternative turnaround

alternative trail

Los Pinos Trail

Los Pinos Peak 4,510 ft.

N

0   0.5   1

Miles

less-traveled Trabuco Canyon has a feeling of remoteness and a primitive character seldom found on such a short hike.

Unlike Holy Jim Canyon, there is no waterfall on the Trabuco Trail to attract the crowds. But the area is more open and affords better views into the surrounding mountain terrain. The spring wildflower displays along Trabuco Creek are some of the finest in the entire Santa Ana range. Most of the trail is exposed to direct sun, so pick a cooler day for this hike.

After leaving the parking area, the nice footpath heads under large oak trees, then into more open terrain alongside Trabuco Creek. The trail crosses the creekbed a few times, then closely follows the left (north) side of the creek. In spring, the next mile or so of trail is bounded by many varieties of wildflowers.

The trail passes near an old mine entrance in the hillside. Yeager Mesa, a private inholding and pristine oak-surrounded meadow, is on the right (south) side of the creek at 0.9 mile. Eventually, the trail passes into the shade of trees along the creek. Under a tree canopy at 1.8 miles, you reach a sign marking the split of the Trabuco Trail, which crosses the stream to the right (south), and the West Horsethief Trail, which climbs up switchbacks on the left (north). A sign marks this juncture. This is a nice place to picnic and enjoy the shaded quiet.

After relaxing, return to your car the way you came.

Options: You can lengthen this hike by choosing either of two options. From the juncture of the Trabuco and West Horsethief Trails, cross the stream to your right (south) and pick up the Trabuco Trail again. The Trabuco Trail gradually rises up the canyon above the creek. At the 3.3-mile mark, the trail appears to split on the ridge; stay right. Soon, the path becomes very shaded, and at 4.4 miles, you arrive at the Main Divide Road. Either return the way you came (an 8.8-mile round-trip hike), or continue from this trail intersection by following a footpath, the Los Pinos Trail, that heads right (south) from the junction. Follow the trail along the ridge for 1.1 miles to the 4,510-foot summit of Los Pinos Peak (Hike 22), and enjoy the spectacular view. Return the way you came.

20
SAN JUAN LOOP TRAIL

Type of hike: Loop.
Total distance: 2.2 miles.
Elevation gain: 320 feet.
Topo map: USGS Sitton Peak.
Jurisdiction: Cleveland National Forest.
Permits: A Forest Adventure Pass is required.
Finding the trailhead: From Interstate 5 (the Santa Ana Freeway) in San Juan Capistrano, drive approximately 19.5 miles east on the Ortega Highway (California 74). At this point, you see the Ortega Oaks Country Store on your right (east). Park across the highway in a USDA Forest Service parking area. The trail begins on the right (north) side of the parking area, near the access to the highway.

Key points:
0.2 Pass small falls and water pools.
1.2 Reach the junction of the Chiquito Trail and stay left (southwest).
1.5 Pass behind the Upper San Juan Campground.
2.2 Return to the parking area.

The hike: This trail takes you to a variety of coastal mountain habitats, including seasonal waterfalls, dense mature oak woodlands, and open chaparral-covered hillsides. Though

San Juan Loop Trail

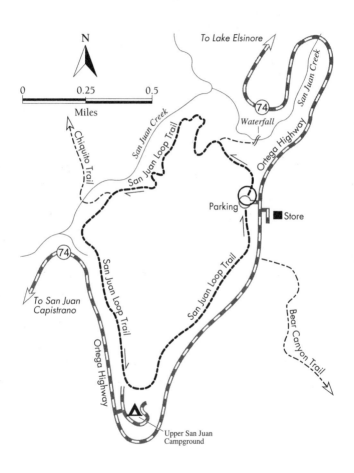

best tackled in the cooler months, an early morning start in the summer is bound to be pleasant and will allow you to see birds and animals when they are most active.

Six mountain streams merge along this short hike, forming San Juan Creek, a major county waterway. San Juan Creek flows west to join Trabuco Creek at the Mission San Juan Capistrano. The granite rocks that line the narrow canyons and dot the hillsides extend southeast through the San Mateo Wilderness. San Juan Canyon was a traditional Native American travel route over the Santa Ana Mountains and through the dense chaparral.

Start your hike on the right (north) side of the parking area. The trail begins with a slight climb, but soon you begin to descend into a rocky canyon. A spur trail on your right makes a short, but worthwhile, side trip to a seasonal waterfall and rock pools at 0.2 mile. Visit the falls, then continue down the main trail along a series of switchbacks until the trail straightens and levels.

Proceed under a canopy of old oaks along the side of the stream until you reach the junction with the Chiquito Trail at 1.2 miles. Stay to the left and continue on the pleasant, shady trail to Upper San Juan Campground. Again, stay left, passing behind the campground at 1.5 miles, and follow a wide section of trail that climbs back into more open terrain. A gentle but constant climb eventually brings you back to the west end of the parking area at 2.2 miles.

21
BEAR CANYON TRAIL

Type of hike: Out-and-back.
Total distance: 4 miles.
Elevation gain: 720 feet.
Topo map: USGS Sitton Peak.
Jurisdiction: San Mateo Canyon Wilderness Area, Cleveland National Forest.
Permits: A Forest Adventure Pass is required.
Finding the trailhead: From Interstate 5 (the Santa Ana Freeway) in San Juan Capistrano, drive approximately 19.5 miles east on the Ortega Highway (California 74). At this point, the Ortega Oaks Country Store is on your right (east). Park across the highway in a USDA Forest Service parking area; this is also the parking area for the San Juan Loop Trail (Hike 20). The trail begins on the east side of the highway, about 75 yards southwest of the store.

Key points:
0.8 Cross a seasonal stream.
1.0 Arrive at the Morgan Trail junction.
2.0 Reach the crest of the hill.

The hike: Like many Santa Ana Mountains hikes, the Bear Canyon Trail is best in the cooler spring, fall, or winter months. Only portions of the trail pass under ancient stands

Bear Canyon Trail

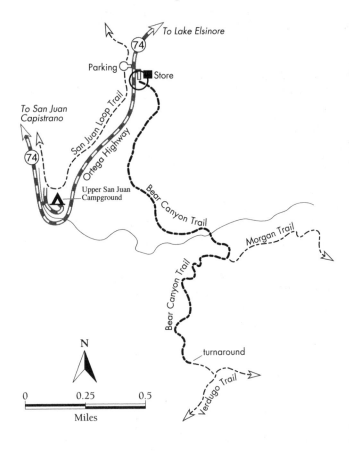

of oak trees; most of the hike proceeds along exposed chaparral-covered hillsides.

This trail takes you from the busy Ortega Highway corridor into the San Mateo Canyon Wilderness. Incredible vistas of some of the wildest sections of the Santa Ana Mountains are your reward. Despite the relatively short nature of the hike, you very quickly lose all signs of civilization.

The Bear Canyon Trail is also a great way to familiarize yourself with some of the natural history of the Santa Ana Mountains. Picnic tables outside the Ortega Oaks Country Store make a great place to relax at the end of your journey.

From the trailhead, walk a short distance to a backcountry registration station and sign in. From here, the trail climbs up and right (east) along the open hillside, eventually crossing under a granite pinnacle.

Continue up along the hillside through decomposing granite until the trail levels. The highway is now lost to view and out of earshot, and the going is largely flat, with views to open chaparral-laden hillsides. Cross a seasonal stream at 0.8 mile, then pass a wilderness boundary sign and into the shade of oak and sycamore trees.

Continue under the trees along the valley bottom until you reach the junction with the Morgan Trail at 1 mile. Head right, staying on the Bear Canyon Trail as it begins a climb up the hillside. At the crest of the hill at 2 miles, enjoy the views to the south and west into the depths of the San Mateo Canyon Wilderness.

Return along the same route, making sure to turn left at the Morgan Trail junction. The mostly downhill trek back to the trailhead goes quickly.

22
LOS PINOS PEAK

Type of hike: Out-and-back.
Total distance: 4.4 miles.
Elevation gain: 920 feet.
Topo map: USGS Alberhill.
Jurisdiction: Cleveland National Forest.
Permits: A Forest Adventure Pass is required.
Finding the trailhead: From Interstate 5 (the Santa Ana Freeway), take the Ortega Highway (California 74) east for 21.9 miles to Long Canyon Road. Turn left (north), and follow this paved road for 3.5 miles (passing the entrance to Bluejay Campground) until you reach Main Divide Road. Make a sharp left (west) and drive 0.5 mile up Main Divide Road to a metal gate. Park off to the right (east), taking care not to block the gate or the road. If the gate is open, you may shorten the hike by 1.1 miles by driving to the Los Pinos Saddle.

Key points:
1.1 Reach the junction of the Los Pinos Trail and Main Divide Road.
2.2 Reach the summit of Los Pinos Peak.

The hike: At 4,510 feet, Los Pinos Peak is the fourth highest summit in the Santa Ana Mountains, yet it is one of the wildest and least visited of the range's high points. Never-

Los Pinos Peak

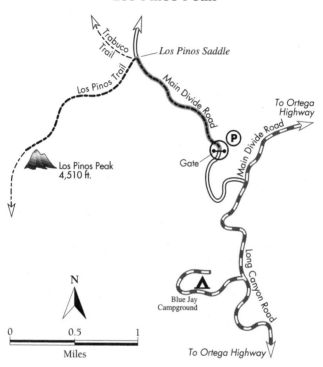

Trabuco Trail

Los Pinos Saddle

Los Pinos Trail

Main Divide Road

To Ortega Highway

Main Divide Road

P

Gate

Los Pinos Peak
4,510 ft.

N

0   0.5   1

Miles

Blue Jay
Campground

Long Canyon Road

To Ortega Highway

theless, Los Pinos lies within easy reach of the more deter-
mined hiker, who will be rewarded with one of the best vistas in Southern California. On clear days, you can look westward across miles of mountains, foothills, and valleys to the
Pacific Ocean. To the east lies Lake Elsinore, with the high
peaks of the San Jacinto and San Gabriel Mountains rising

in the distance. On spring days wildflowers, green hillsides, and the snow-covered peaks of distant mountains are common sights. Summer can be brutally hot, and winter storms may bring a light covering of snow to Los Pinos.

From the gate, begin hiking up the dirt Main Divide fire road. As you ascend along the west and east sides of the mountain ridge, you begin to gain good views as well as elevation. Continue up the fire road until you reach Los Pinos Saddle, a large flat area with several metal guardrails.

The Los Pinos and Trabuco Trails join Main Divide Road on your left (west) at 1.1 miles. Start the Los Pinos Trail where the Trabuco Trail hits Main Divide Road, but head up the path on the left (south). The Los Pinos Trail winds around the north and west sides of the hillside, eventually joining the exposed ridge.

Continue to gain elevation up the wide ridge trail to a high point (4,489 feet). From here, the ridge trail dips slightly, then gains a bit to eventually reach the top of Los Pinos Peak (4,510 feet) at 2.2 miles. Soak up the view and look for the U.S. Geological Survey benchmarks on the rocky summit just south of the trail. Turn around and return the way you came, gliding downhill to your car.

23
EL CARISO NATURE TRAIL

Type of hike: Loop.
Total distance: 1.4 miles.
Elevation gain: 120 feet.
Topo map: USGS Alberhill.
Jurisdiction: Cleveland National Forest.
Permits: A Forest Adventure Pass is not required.
Finding the trailhead: From Interstate 5 (the Santa Ana Freeway) in San Juan Capistrano, drive approximately 23.1 miles east on the Ortega Highway (California 74) until you reach the El Cariso Ranger Station, which is on the right (south). Parking is available directly in front of the visitor center. If this parking lot is full, park in the lot across the highway. The trail begins immediately to the right of the visitor center.

Key points:
0.4 Pass the Old Mine Prospect Tunnel.
1.2 Cross Main Divide Road a second time.

The hike: El Cariso Nature Trail is an ideal short family hike. With striking vistas to the north, west, and south, it winds around a large knoll above the El Cariso Ranger Station, which is just south of the Ortega Highway. The trail is a great way to familiarize yourself with some of the natural history of the Santa Ana Mountains. Stop at the small visitor center and, if available, take a trail pamphlet that is co-

El Cariso Nature Trail

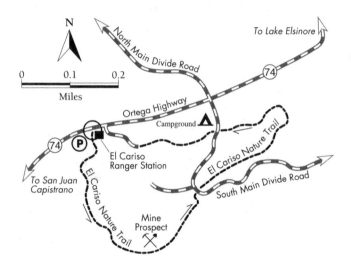

ordinated with numbered markers found along the trail. This pamphlet will help you identify some of the plants, animals, and geologic features of this coastal mountain range.

In the spring, a variety of wildflowers can be observed, along with a wide variety of coastal shrubs. The Coulter pines (called "penny pines") have been planted over the years, and are native to the area. Though some shade will be found, most of the hike is exposed to the sun. You should avoid hot summer days, or start early in the morning.

A small shaded area with tables is located at the trailhead, behind the visitor center; this is a perfect spot for a picnic.

The trail begins as a dirt path on the west (right) side of the visitor center. Head up stone steps, then proceed uphill under the oaks. Almost immediately, you break out into scrub oak and coastal sage, and head up a few short switchbacks.

Beyond a bench, the trail follows the contours of the western slope of the hill, and offers expansive vistas. The trail climbs slightly and heads up a short section of stone steps. As the trail winds around to the southern side of the hillside, note the acorn-bearing scrub oak, which was a valuable food source for Native Americans.

At 0.4 mile (signpost 10), an interesting old mine prospect and tunnel head into the hillside. To the south, you can gaze into the San Mateo Canyon Wilderness. The trail heads east, eventually reaching and crossing the paved Main Divide Road. The trail continues east into scattered stands of Coulter pines and brings you to signpost 12.

Intermittent shade and sun are encountered as the trail turns north, then west, reaching and crossing Main Divide Road a second time at 1.2 miles. More open terrain behind picnic areas leads to a paved storage area. Continue across the storage area to your car and the starting point.

24
MORGAN TRAIL

Type of hike: Out-and-back.
Total distance: 4.5 miles.
Elevation gain: 500 feet.
Topo maps: USGS Alberhill and Sitton Peak.
Jurisdiction: Cleveland National Forest.
Permits: A Forest Adventure Pass is required.
Finding the trailhead: From Interstate 5 (the Santa Ana Freeway) in San Juan Capistrano, drive approximately 23.4 miles east on the Ortega Highway (California 74) until you reach Killen Trail Road (South Main Divide Road). Turn right (southeast) and drive 2.5 miles to the Morgan Trail parking area, which is on your right (south).

Key points:
0.2 Reach Morrell Canyon Creek.
1.2 Cross Morrell Canyon Creek.
1.5 Arrive at a picnic area on flat rocks.
2.2 Reach the fence line and turnaround point.

The hike: Like the Bear Canyon Trail (Hike 21), the Morgan Trail takes you into the San Mateo Canyon Wilderness Area in the southern part of the Santa Ana Mountains. In fact, with a car shuttle between the Morgan and Bear Canyon Trailheads, you could make a point-to-point hike of 5.1 miles.

Morgan Trail

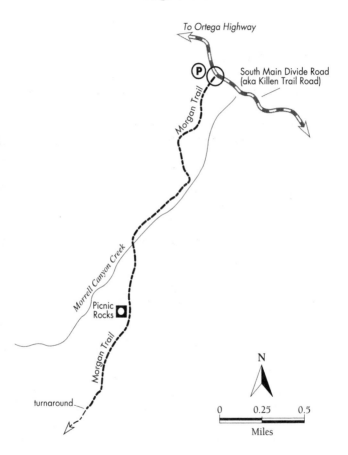

The trail offers a great deal of variety for a short wilderness hike. The Morgan Trail takes you from open chaparral to the shade of oaks, sycamores, and willows along Morrell Canyon Creek, then back up to views toward Sitton Peak in the west. Along the banks of Morrell Canyon Creek, large boulders and grassy areas shaded by ancient oak trees provide ideal spots for wildlife watching, sitting, daydreaming, or picnicking.

From the small parking area, head southwest as the trail gradually descends. After a short distance, you will encounter a backcountry registration station.

The trail continues a slight descent, and at 0.2 mile you reach an oak woodland along Morrell Canyon Creek. Continue downstream on gentle rolling terrain along the right (northwest) side of Morrell Canyon under the shade of oaks that often arch across the trail. Note the many fire-scorched tree trunks.

As the canyon deepens, you will pass many granite rocks and boulders. The trail slowly enters more open terrain and crosses Morrell Canyon Creek at 1.2 miles. Continue along the opposite side of the creek in open chaparral as the trail rolls slightly up and down. Some flat rocks on your right at 1.5 miles make a nice spot for a picnic, with open vistas to the west.

The trail heads down a moderate grade along a wide-open ridge toward the more level "poterra," a Spanish word for a flat and open meadow. The trail levels and heads over some small ridges. At 2.2 miles, a fenceline and old fire road are encountered. Turn around at the fence, and follow the Morgan Trail back the way you came.